National 5
Lifeskills
Maths

Practice Papers for SQA Exams

Robert Barclay

Contents

 HODDER GIBSON
AN HACHETTE UK COMPANY

The Publishers would like to thank the following for permission to reproduce copyright material:

Exam rubric in Paper 1 and Paper 2 of each practice paper; Formulae list, Copyright © Scottish Qualifications Authority.

Acknowledgements

Every effort has been made to trace all copyright holders, but if any have been inadvertently overlooked the Publishers will be pleased to make the necessary arrangements at the first opportunity.

Although every effort has been made to ensure that website addresses are correct at time of going to press, Hodder Gibson cannot be held responsible for the content of any website mentioned in this book. It is sometimes possible to find a relocated web page by typing in the address of the home page for a website in the URL window of your browser.

Hachette UK's policy is to use papers that are natural, renewable and recyclable products and made from wood grown in sustainable forests. The logging and manufacturing processes are expected to conform to the environmental regulations of the country of origin.

Orders: please contact Bookpoint Ltd, 130 Park Drive, Milton Park, Abingdon, Oxon OX14 4SE. Telephone: (44) 01235 827720. Fax: (44) 01235 400454. Lines are open 9.00–5.00, Monday to Saturday, with a 24-hour message answering service. Visit our website at www.hoddereducation.co.uk. Hodder Gibson can be contacted direct on: Tel: 0141 333 4650; Fax: 0141 404 8188; email: hoddergibson@hodder.co.uk

© Robert Barclay 2016
First published in 2016 by
Hodder Gibson, an imprint of Hodder Education,
An Hachette UK Company
211 St Vincent Street
Glasgow G2 5QY

Impression number   5 4 3 2 1
Year   2020 2019 2018 2017 2016

Cover photo © Thinkstock
Illustrations by Aptara, Inc.
Typeset in Din Regular, 12/14.4 pts. by Aptara, Inc.
Printed in Great Britain by CPI Group (UK) Ltd, Croydon, CR0 4YY

A catalogue record for this title is available from the British Library

ISBN: 978 1 4718 8602 7

Introduction

National 5 Lifeskills Maths

The course

The Lifeskills Mathematics course focuses on the application of mathematical reasoning skills, linked to real-life contexts. You will be asked to analyse, compare, justify and communicate information.

Learners following this course are expected to have already attained the knowledge, understanding and skills required to pass the National 4 Lifeskills Mathematics course and/or be proficient in equivalent experiences and outcomes.

The course comprises three component Units: Managing Finance & Statistics, Geometry & Measures and Numeracy, and the Course assessment i.e. the examination.

An overview of the course coverage is given in the table below.

Managing Finance & Statistics	Geometry & Measures	Numeracy
Financial Skills:	**Geometrical Skills:**	**Numerical Skills:**
Budgeting	Gradient	Whole number and decimal calculations
Income	Perimeter and area of composite shapes	Rounding
Best deal	Volume of composite solids	Fractions and mixed numbers
Foreign currency	Pythagoras' theorem	Percentages (including compound)
Borrowing and saving	**Measurement Skills:**	Distance, speed and time
Statistical Skills:	Calculating a quantity based on two related pieces of information	Perimeter and circumference
Statistical graphs, charts and diagrams	Scale drawing (including bearings)	Area
Averages and measures of spread	Container packing	Volume
	Precedence tables	Ratio
	Time	Proportion
	Tolerance	Reading scales
		Interpreting data:
		Statistical graphs, charts and diagrams
		Probability

Assessment

To gain the course award, you must pass the three Units as well as the examination. The Units are assessed internally on a pass/fail basis and the examination is set and marked externally by SQA. It tests skills beyond the minimum competence required for the Units. The course award is graded A–D, the grade being determined by the total mark you score in the examination.

The number of marks, allotted times and a description of the types of questions in the examination papers are as follows:

Paper	Marks	Time	Types of Questions
Paper 1	35	50 minutes	You may NOT use a calculator. A mixture of short, medium and extended questions which can cover one skill within a Unit to three or four skills from across the Units.
Paper 2	55	1 hour 40 minutes	You may use a calculator. A mixture of short, medium and extended case studies. Each will follow a theme and can cover one skill within a Unit to three or more from across the Units.

The papers are 'structured' which means that you write your answer on the exam paper next to the question. This gives you the advantage of being able to complete tables, draw on graphs and annotate diagrams, without having to draw them yourself.

Some tips for achieving a good mark

- **DOING** maths questions is the most effective use of your study time. You will benefit much more from spending 30 minutes doing maths questions than spending several hours copying out notes or reading a maths textbook.
- Practise doing the types of questions that are likely to appear in the exam. Use the marking instructions to check your answers and to understand what the examiners are looking for. Ask your teacher for help if you get stuck.
- **SHOW ALL WORKING CLEARLY.** The instructions on the front of the exam paper state that 'Full credit will only be given where the solution contains appropriate working'. A 'correct' answer with no working may only be awarded partial marks or even no marks at all. An incomplete answer will be awarded marks for any appropriate working. Attempt every question, even if you are not sure whether you are correct or not. Your solution may contain working which will gain some marks. A blank response is certain to be awarded no marks. Never score out working unless you have something better to replace it with.
- Reasoning skills are a major part of Lifeskills Mathematics. One way of showing your reasoning process is by showing all of your working. Quite often you will be asked to 'Use your working to justify your answer' – so you cannot just say 'yes' or 'no' without showing your working.
- Communication is very important in presenting solutions to questions. Diagrams are often a good way of conveying information and enabling markers to understand your working. Where a diagram is included in a question, it is often good practice to mark in any dimensions etc. which you work out and may use later.

- Remember to **state units**, where appropriate. In many questions the mark for the final answer is only given if the correct units are stated.
- In Paper 1, you have to carry out calculations without a calculator. Ensure that you practise your number skills regularly, especially within questions that test course content.
- In Paper 2, you will be allowed to use a calculator. Always use your own calculator. Different calculators often function in slightly different ways, so make sure that you know how to operate yours. Having to use a calculator that you are unfamiliar with on the day of the exam may cause frustration and waste valuable time.
- Prepare thoroughly to tackle questions from all parts of the course. Always try all parts of a question. Just because you could not complete part (a), for example, does not mean you could not do part (b) or (c).
- Look at how many marks are allocated to a question – this will give you an idea of how much work is required.The more marks, the more work!
- By working through these practice papers you will get a feel for the type and variety of questions you could be asked and you will therefore be better prepared to do well in the examination.

Revision grid

	Practice Paper A		Practice Paper B		Practice Paper C	
	Paper 1	**Paper 2**	**Paper 1**	**Paper 2**	**Paper 1**	**Paper 2**
Budgeting			Q4		Q5, 7	
Income		Q1		Q3	Q5	
Determine the best deal		Q5	Q8a	Q7b,c		Q4b
Foreign exchange		Q3		Q5a,b		Q4
Borrowing and saving				Q1		Q2, 4b
Compound percentage increase and decrease	Q8					
Percentages		Q1a, 2a,c	Q4	Q1, 3, 4b, 5a	Q7	Q2, 3c, 4b, 5b
Fractions			Q5		Q5	Q1a
Statistical diagrams	Q3	Q7	Q9	Q4a,c	Q4, 8	
Statistics		Q7	Q9	Q2	Q8	Q6
Probability	Q4	Q7b,c	Q2			
Calculating a quantity based on several related pieces of information	Q6			Q6c		Q3c, 5b
Distance, speed and time	Q2	Q4c		Q5c, 6b	Q3	Q1a
Scale drawing		Q4a,b	Q10			Q5a
Container packing		Q2b	Q8b			
Precedence tables	Q5		Q7			
Tolerance	Q4		Q1		Q2	
Perimeter		Q6c				Q1b
Area		Q6a,b	Q6			Q3b
Volume	Q9	Q2a,c		Q7d,e	Q9c	Q7
Pythagoras' Theorem	Q9			Q6b	Q9a	
Gradient	Q7			Q6a	Q9b	
Rounding		Q2a, 4c, 6b		Q5c, 6b, 7e		Q2b, 7
Ratio				Q7a	Q6	Q3a
Proportion			Q3		Q1	
Reading scales	Q1		Q1		Q8	

National 5
Lifeskills Maths

HODDER
GIBSON
LEARN MORE

Formulae list

Circumference of a circle: $C = \pi d$

Area of a circle: $A = \pi r^2$

Theorem of Pythagoras: 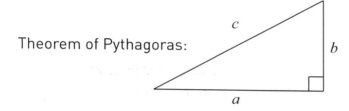 $a^2 + b^2 = c^2$

Volume of a cylinder: $V = \pi r^2 h$

Volume of a prism: $V = Ah$

Volume of a cone: $V = \frac{1}{3}\pi r^2 h$

Volume of a sphere: $V = \frac{4}{3}\pi r^3$

Standard deviation: $s = \sqrt{\dfrac{\Sigma(x - \bar{x})^2}{n-1}} = \sqrt{\dfrac{\Sigma x^2 - (\Sigma x)^2/n}{n-1}}$, where n is the sample size.

Gradient: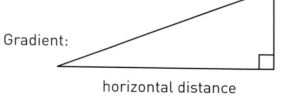

$$\text{gradient} = \frac{\text{vertical height}}{\text{horizontal distance}}$$

Paper 1 (non-calculator)

Total marks: 35

Attempt ALL questions.

You may NOT use a calculator.

Full credit will be given only to solutions which contain appropriate working.

State the units for your answer where appropriate.

Write your answers in the spaces provided in this booklet. Additional space for answers is provided at the end of this booklet. If you use this space you must clearly identify the question number you are attempting.

Use **blue** or **black** ink.

MARKS

1 Jenny takes a solid silver bowl to a dealer to have it valued.

The dealer values the bowl according to its weight.

He values it at 30 pence per gram.

The scales below show the weight of Jenny's bowl.

1.7 kg

$$\begin{array}{r} 1700\,g \\ \times \quad 30 \\ \hline \pounds 510 \end{array}$$

£510

2

What value does the dealer place on Jenny's bowl?

MARKS

2. An overnight train travelled from Aberdeen to London at an average speed of 120 kilometres per hour.

   It left Aberdeen at 2253 and arrived in London at 0611.

   Calculate the distance travelled by the train from Aberdeen to London.

   3

   2253 → 2300 → 0600 → 0611
   7min   7hr   11min

   7hrs 18 min

   $D = S \times T$
   $= 120 \times 7.3$
   $= 876 k$

   60)18 = .3

   120.0
   × 7.3
   3600
   8400

3. The table shows the number of units of electricity used in heating a house on ten different days and the average temperature for each day.

Units of electricity used	7	3	1	7	4	6	11	9	10	13
Average temperature (°C)	10	20	23	16	13	13	4	7	5	4

   a) Plot this information on a scattergraph.

   (An additional graph grid, if required, can be found on *Page 10*)

   2

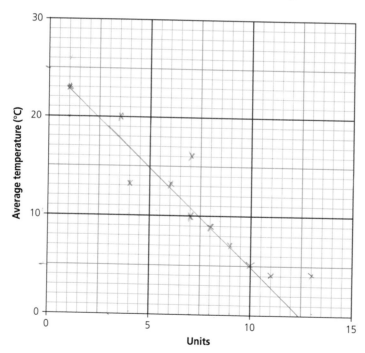

   b) Draw a line of best fit on your scattergraph.

   1

   c) Use your line of best fit to estimate the temperature if 8 units of electricity are used. *9°*

   1

4 A machine produces bolts which are required to have a diameter of 4·3 ± 0·05 mm.

Listed below are the diameters, in mm, of a sample of bolts produced by the machine.

4·35 4·28 4·33 4·29 4·30 4·34 4·25 4·26 4·36 4·30

4·27 4·31 4·32 4·24 4·35 4·40 4·35 4·30 4·29 4·32

a) What is the probability that a bolt chosen at random from this sample will have a diameter within the required limits?

lower limit = 4·25 $\frac{17}{20}$

upper limit = 4·35

b) The machine produces ten thousand bolts each day.

Calculate an estimate of how many bolts will have a diameter within the required limits.

500 × 17

20 ⟌ 10000

```
  500
×  17
 3500
  500
 8500
```

8500 bolts will have diameter within required limits

5   A construction company is going to build an extension to a house.

     The table below shows the list of tasks involved in the construction
     of the extension and the time required for each.

Task	Detail	Preceding task	Time (days)
A	Dig foundations, pour concrete and wait to set	None	5
B	Build walls	A	4
C	Install roof and ceiling	B	2
D	Fit doors and windows	C	2
E	Install electrical wiring	C	1
F	Install central heating	C	1
G	Lay floor	E, F	1
H	Plaster interior walls and wait to dry	G	5
I	Paint interior walls and ceiling	H	1
J	Roughcast exterior walls	D	2

MARKS

a) Complete the diagram below by writing these tasks and times in the
   appropriate boxes.

   (An additional diagram, if required, can be found on *Page 11*)

2

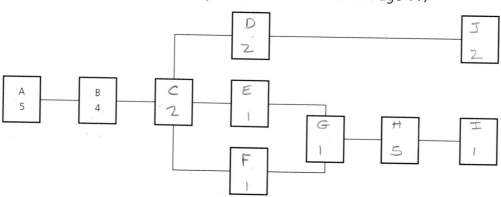

b) The construction company claims it can construct the extension in
   four weeks if it works Monday to Friday each week. Is this a valid claim?
   Give a reason for your answer.

2

A→B→C→E→G→H→I

5+4+2+ +1+5+1 = 19 days

MARKS

6 Mary drives 700 miles from Aberdeen to York and back.

Calculate the cost of the petrol for Mary's journey given that

- the average petrol consumption for the journey was 35 miles per gallon
- petrol costs £1·10 per litre
- 1 gallon = 4·55 litres.

3

35⟌700   20 gallons

4·55
× 20
91·00 ltrs

20 gallons = 91 litres
£91 + 9·10
= £100·10

7 The diagrams below show the side views of two buildings.

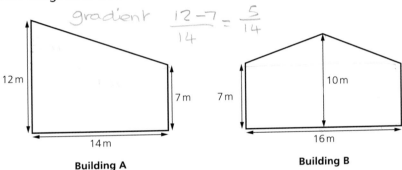

gradient $\frac{12-7}{14} = \frac{5}{14}$

12m   7m   7m   10m

14m   16m

Building A   **Building B**

The side view of

- Building A consists of a rectangle and a right-angled triangle
- Building B consists of a rectangle and an isosceles triangle.

a) Find the gradient of the roof of Building A.

1

$$\frac{5}{14}$$

b) Is the roof of Building B steeper than that of Building A?
Justify your answer.

3

Ⓑ $\frac{10-7}{8} = \frac{3}{8} + \frac{3 \times 7}{8 \times 7} = \frac{21}{56}$

Ⓐ $\frac{5 \times 4}{14 \times 4} = \frac{20}{56}$

yes because $\frac{21}{56}$ is greater than $\frac{20}{56}$

8 Andy buys a car for £14 000.

MARKS

The value of the car depreciates by 20% per annum.

Andy will sell the car at the end of the year in which its value falls below half of the amount he paid for it.

After how many years should Andy sell the car?

You must explain your answer.   7000

4

1.   14000 − 20% = 2800

2.   11 200 − 20% = 2240

3.   8960 − 20% = 1792

4.   £7168 − 20% = 1433.60
      5734.40

he will sell in year 4

896
896
1792

716·8
716·8
1433·6

11200
2240
8960
1792
7168
1433·6
5734·4

9 The pyramid below has a rectangular base of length 6 centimetres and breadth 8 centimetres. Each sloping edge is 13 centimetres long.

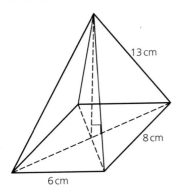

The volume of a pyramid is given by the formula

$$V = \frac{1}{3}Ah$$

where A is the area of its base and h is its height.

Calculate the volume of the above pyramid.

6

$d^2 = 6^2 + 8^2 \quad (d = \text{diagonal})$

$d^2 = 36 + 64$

$d = \sqrt{100}$

$d = 10.$

$h^2 = 13^2 - 5^2$

$h^2 = 169 - 25$

$h = \sqrt{144}$

$h = 12$

$\begin{array}{r} 13 \\ 13 \\ \hline 39 \\ 13 \\ \hline 169 \end{array}$
$\begin{array}{r} 169 \\ -\ 25 \\ \hline 144 \end{array}$

$V = \frac{1}{3} \times (6 \times 8) \times 12$

$V = \frac{1}{3} \times 48 \times 12$

$V = \frac{1}{3} 576$

$V = 192 \, cm^3$

$\begin{array}{r} 48 \\ 12 \\ \hline 96 \\ 48 \\ \hline 576 \end{array}$

[End of Paper 1]

ADDITIONAL SPACE FOR ANSWERS

Additional graph grid for Question 3a)

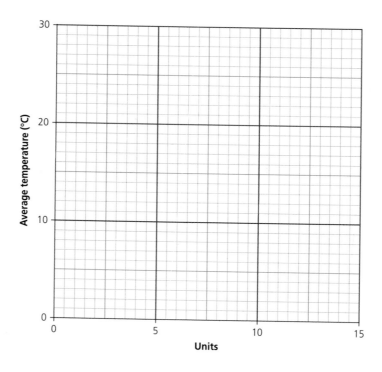

ADDITIONAL SPACE FOR ANSWERS

Additional diagram for Question 5a)

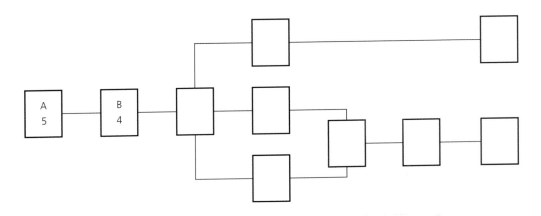

A

ADDITIONAL SPACE FOR ANSWERS

Paper 2 (calculator)

Total marks: 55

Attempt ALL questions.

You may use a calculator.

Full credit will be given only to solutions which contain appropriate working.

State the units for your answer where appropriate.

Write your answers clearly in the spaces provided in this booklet. Additional space for answers is provided at the end of this booklet. If you use this space you must clearly identify the question number you are attempting.

Use **blue** or **black** ink.

MARKS

1 Jim Oliver earned £43 800 last year.

His personal tax allowance was £10 740.

The rates of tax applicable were as follows.

Taxable income	Rate
On the first £31 875	20%
On the next £118 215	40%
On any income over £150 000	45%

a) How much tax did he pay last year?

4

b) Jim also paid £343·20 **per month** in National Insurance and £273·75 **per month** into his pension.

Calculate Jim's **monthly** take-home pay.

3

43800 − 10740
= 33060

31 875 × 0.2 = 6375
33060 − 31 875 = 1185 × 0.4
= 474

a) £6849 tax
b) 4118.40 NI
   3285 pension

Gross pay £43800·00
− deductions 14 252·40
Net pay 29 547·60
per month (29547·60 ÷ 12) = £2462·30

2 A cylindrical can has diameter 8·2 centimetres and height 10 centimetres.

radius 4·1

10 cm

8.2 cm

The can is filled with cola to 95% of its capacity.

a) Calculate the volume of cola in the can.

Give your answer correct to 3 significant figures.

3

$$V = \pi r^2 h$$
$$= \pi \, 4 \cdot 1^2 \, h$$
$$= 528 \cdot 10 \, cm^3 \checkmark$$

$$0.95 \times 528 \cdot 1 = 501 \cdot 69$$
$$= 502 \, cm^3 \checkmark$$

Cans like the one above are to be stored in a mini fridge.

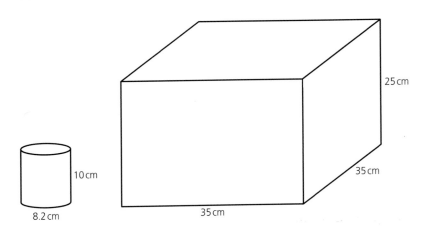

25 cm

35 cm

10 cm

35 cm

8.2 cm

The mini fridge is a cuboid with internal dimensions 35 centimetres by 35 centimetres by 25 centimetres.

b) What is the maximum number of these cans that can be stored in the mini fridge?

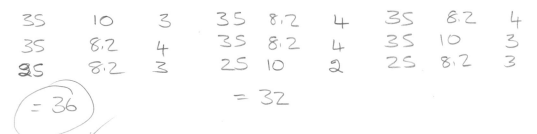

35	10	3		35	8.2	4		35	8.2	4
35	8.2	4		35	8.2	4		35	10	3
25	8.2	3		25	10	2		25	8.2	3

= 36 ✓   = 32

c) Express the volume occupied by the number of cans in (b) as a percentage of the total volume of the mini fridge.

$V = \pi r^2 h$
$= \pi \times 4.1^2 \times 10$
$= \pi \times 16.81 \times 10$
$= 528.1 cm^3$

$V = Lbh$
$= 35 \times 35 \times 25$
$= 30625 cm^3$

528.1×36

$= \dfrac{19012}{30625} \times 100$?

$= 62\%$

A

3 George is in the duty-free shop at Prague airport (Czech Republic).

He sees a camera for CZK3000.

He does not have any Czech Koruna so he hands over Đ100 and £20.

He receives his change in Czech Koruna.

Currency	Exchange rate
Czech Koruna	£1 = CZK32·71
Euro	£1 = Đ1·38

How much change does he receive?

3

$£20 = 20 \times 32.71$

$= CZK\ 654.20$

$Đ100 = 100 \div 1.38 \times 32.71$

$= CZK\ 2370.29$

$+\quad 654.20$

$\overline{\quad\quad 3624.49}$

$-3000.$

$CZK\quad\quad 24.49$

4 A ferry sails 40 kilometres from Ardpoint to Boisdale on a bearing of 060°.

It then sails 55 kilometres from Boisdale to Cairnross on a bearing of 155°.

a) Using a suitable scale, construct a scale drawing to illustrate this journey.

Ardpoint

b) The ferry then sails directly from Cairnross back to Ardpoint.

Find the distance and bearing of Ardpoint from Cairnross.

2

c) The ferry is scheduled to
- depart from Ardpoint at 0940
- stop at Boisdale for 15 minutes
- stop at Cairnross for 15 minutes
- return to Ardpoint at 1730.

Find the average speed that the ferry must sail at in order to return to Ardpoint at the scheduled time.
Give your answer to the nearest kilometre per hour.

3

A

5 The table below shows the cost of three companies' TV, phone and broadband packages.

Company	Connection charge	Package fee	Line rental	Special offers
Teleview	£31·75	£20·00	£16·99	No offer
Scotcall	£55·95	£27·00	£17·99	50% off package fee for the first year.
Cablevision	£49·95	£22·50	£17·50	£10 off package fee for the first 6 months.

The connection charge only applies in the first year of each package.

The package fee and line rental are paid monthly.

a) Calculate the cost for the first year of Cablevision's package.

2

connection charge 49·95
package fee 6 × 12.50 + 6 × 22.50
line rental 12 × 17.50

49.95
210.00
210.00
£469·95 ✓

b) Which company offers the best deal for the first year of the package? Show working to justify your answer.

4

Teleview 31.75 + (12 × £20) + (12 × 16.99) = £475.63 ✓
Scotcall 55.95 + (12 × 13.50) + (12 × 17.99) = £433.83 ✓

Scotcall.

c) Which company offers the best deal from the second year onwards? Justify your answer.

1

2nd yr Teleview 475.63 − 31.75   £443.88
Scotcall 433.83 − 55.95 + (12 × 13.50) = £564.08
Cablevision 469.95 − 49.95 + (6 × 12.50) = 495.00

6 Bill is making a wooden worktop for his kitchen.

The diagram below shows a sketch of how the finished worktop will look.

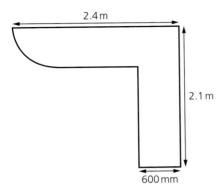

a) He buys the two rectangular lengths of wood shown below from a DIY store.

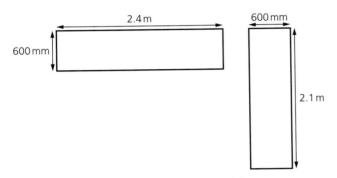

The store charges £49·99 per square metre for the wood.
How much does Bill pay for the two lengths of wood?

2

b) Before joining the two lengths together to make the worktop, Bill cuts off three pieces as shown in the diagram below.

MARKS

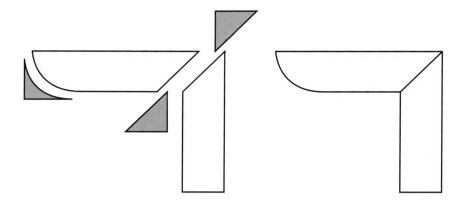

He cuts off:

- a triangular piece from an end of **each** length, in order to make a neat join
- a second piece from the other end of one length, in order to make that end of the worktop a quarter-circle.

Calculate the total area of wood which Bill cuts off.

Give your answer correct to two decimal places.

3

c) Bill attaches a protective edging strip to the edges of the worktop running from A to B to C to D.

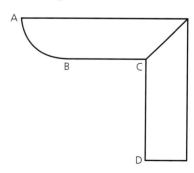

What length of edging strip will he need?

3

7 The stem and leaf diagram below shows the ages of Westfield Football Club's first team squad.

AGES

```
1 | 8  9
2 | 1  2  4  5  5  6  7  9
3 | 0  1  1  3  5  6
4 | 0
```

$n = 17$ 2|1 represents 21 years

a) **(i)** State:

the median age   27
the lower quartile   23
the upper quartile   32

2

(ii) Draw a boxplot to illustrate this data.

2

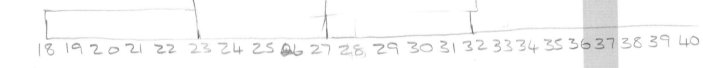

18 19 20 21 22 23 24 25 26 27 28 29 30 31 32 33 34 35 36 37 38 39 40

b) A 'man of the match' is chosen after each game the team plays. What is the probability that the chosen 'man of the match' after one of the games is at least 33 years old?

1

$$\frac{4}{17}$$

c) The boxplot below illustrates the ages of Westfield Football Club's second team squad.

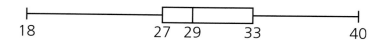

18   27   29   33   40

A 'man of the match' is also chosen after each game the second team plays.

Is the probability of the chosen 'man of the match' being at least 33 years old greater for the first team squad or the second team squad?

Justify your answer.

3

d) The heights, in centimetres, of six defenders in the first team squad are given below.

179   187   193   184   185   182

Calculate:

(i) the mean height

(ii) the standard deviation, correct to one decimal place

e) The mean height and standard deviation for the midfielders in the first team squad are 182 centimetres and 6·5 centimetres respectively.

Make two valid comparisons between the heights of the defenders and the midfielders in the first team squad.

[End of Paper 2]

[END OF PRACTICE PAPER A]

National 5
Lifeskills Maths

HODDER
GIBSON
LEARN MORE

Formulae list

Circumference of a circle: $C = \pi d$

Area of a circle: $A = \pi r^2$

Theorem of Pythagoras:

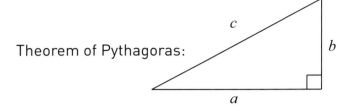

$a^2 + b^2 = c^2$

Volume of a cylinder: $V = \pi r^2 h$

Volume of a prism: $V = Ah$

Volume of a cone: $V = \frac{1}{3}\pi r^2 h$

Volume of a sphere: $V = \frac{4}{3}\pi r^3$

Standard deviation: $s = \sqrt{\dfrac{\Sigma(x - \bar{x})^2}{n-1}} = \sqrt{\dfrac{\Sigma x^2 - (\Sigma x)^2/n}{n-1}}$, where n is the sample size.

Gradient:

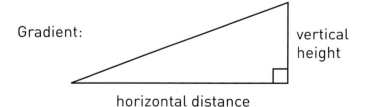

$gradient = \dfrac{vertical\ height}{horizontal\ distance}$

Paper 1 (non-calculator)

Total marks: 35

Attempt ALL questions.

You may NOT use a calculator.

Full credit will be given only to solutions which contain appropriate working.

State the units for your answer where appropriate.

Write your answers in the spaces provided in this booklet. Additional space for answers is provided at the end of this booklet. If you use this space you must clearly identify the question number you are attempting.

Use **blue** or **black** ink.

MARKS

1 A dairy produces small cartons of milk which have a volume of (150 ± 3) ml.

Milk from one carton is poured into the measuring cylinder shown below.

148mL   limits 147/153

148ml is greater than lower limit

Is the volume of milk in this carton within the dairy's acceptable limits?

Justify your answer.

2

2   The table shows the number of pizzas sold by the Pizza Palace one day.

The Pizza Palace					
	Deep Pan		Thin and Crispy		Total
	9-inch	12-inch	9-inch	12-inch	
Margherita	9	4	14	6	33
Hawaii	10	8	13	5	36
Pepperoni	6	2	9	4	21
Total	25	14	36	15	90

What is the probability that a customer chosen at random bought a 9-inch Thin and Crispy pizza?

Give your answer as a fraction in its simplest form.

2

$$\frac{36}{90} \quad \frac{12}{30} \quad \frac{8}{15} \quad \frac{2}{5}$$

3   A shop sells a piece of cheese weighing 360 grams for £2·70.

What is the price of this piece of cheese per kilogram?

2

$$360 = 2.70 \qquad \frac{2.70}{360} \times 1000$$

4   Harry travels regularly between Warren and Cranford by train.

The price of a return ticket for the journey is £26·60.

He buys a RailPass for £40 which entitles him to a 15% discount on the price of each return ticket.

How many return tickets does Harry have to buy for the journey before he recoups the money spent on buying the RailPass?

2

5   Nick is going to bake some loaves of bread.

He needs $\frac{3}{5}$ of a bag of flour for one loaf.

He has 6 bags of flour.

How many loaves can Nick bake?

2

6   ABCD is a square piece of ground of length 60 metres.

A road of width 20 metres passes through the piece of ground.

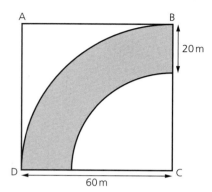

The curved edges of the road are quarter circles with centres at C.

Calculate the area of the road.

(Use π = 3·14)

MARKS

3

7 Jamie is going to cook a meal consisting of chicken in a garlic sauce, vegetables and apple pie.

The table below shows the list of tasks involved and the time required for each.

Task	Detail	Preceding task	Time (minutes)
A	Pre-heat oven	None	10
B	Prepare garlic sauce	None	10
C	Cook chicken in pre-heated oven	A	75
D	Add sauce and complete cooking of chicken	B, C	30
E	Make pastry for apple pie	B	15
F	Prepare apples	E	10
G	Cook apple pie in pre-heated oven	F	40
H	Prepare vegetables	F	20
I	Cook vegetables on hob	H	25
J	Put the food onto plates ready for eating	D, G, I	15

The chicken and the apple pie can both be cooking in the oven at the same time.

a) Complete the diagram below by writing these tasks and times in the appropriate boxes.

(An additional diagram, if required, can be found on *Page 35*)

2

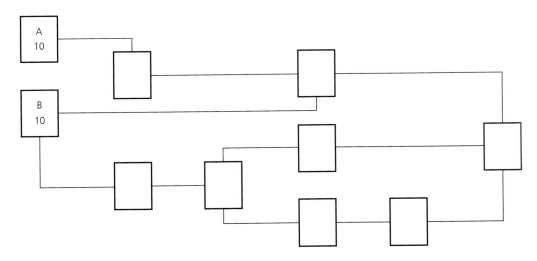

b) Jamie wants to eat the meal at 7.30 pm.

When should he start on the list of tasks involved in making the meal?

2

8 Lindsay wants to send three parcels by a track and sign delivery service.

The parcels weigh 10 kg, 5 kg and 4 kg respectively.

She wants to send them 1st class.

Track and Sign Delivery			
		1st Class	2nd Class
Size	Weight up to and including	Price	Price
Letter	100 g	£1.73	£1.64
Large Letter	100 g	£2.05	£1.84
	250 g	£2.36	£2.29
	500 g	£2.78	£2.61
	750 g	£3.52	£3.15
Small Parcel	1 kg	£4.40	£3.90
	2 kg	£6.55	£3.90
Medium Parcel	1 kg	£6.75	£5.99
	2 kg	£10.00	£5.99
	5 kg	£16.95	£14.85
	10 kg	£23.00	£21.35
	20 kg	£34.50	£29.65

a) Lindsay's parcels are all going to the same address, so she decides to wrap them together and send them as **one** parcel.

How much will she save by sending them as one parcel instead of sending them individually?

3

b) Andrew wants to send twelve parcels by the track and sign delivery service.

He wants to send them 1st class and they are all going to the same address.

The weights of the parcels (in kilograms) are:

14   9   12   7   8   5   4   13   11   5   7   3

To save money, Andrew is going to wrap some of the parcels together to form five larger parcels each weighing 20 kg or less.

Complete the table to show how this can be done.

2

	Weight of individual parcels (kg)	Total weight of parcel (kg)
Parcel 1	14 +	
Parcel 2		
Parcel 3		
Parcel 4		
Parcel 5		

9 The number of hours of sunshine in Lerwick each December during a ten-year period is listed below.

16   20   13   11   28   16   31   24   15   23

a) **(i)** State:

the median number of hours of sunshine

the interquartile range.

(ii) Draw a boxplot to illustrate this data.

b) The boxplot below shows the number of hours of sunshine in Portree each December during the same ten-year period.

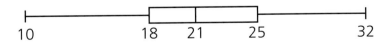

10   18   21   25   32

Make two valid comparisons between the number of hours of sunshine in Lerwick and Portree each December during the ten-year period.

B

10 The scale drawing shows the positions of two airports, Beechwood and Harrison.

Scale: 1 cm represents 40 km

MARKS

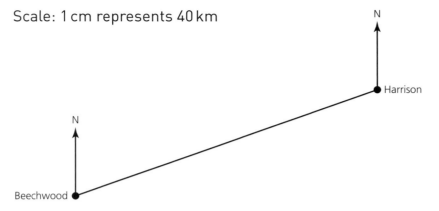

a) Use the scale drawing to find the distance and the bearing of Harrison from Beechwood.

3

b) A third airport, Upton, is on a bearing of 130° from Beechwood. From Harrison its bearing is 215°.
Complete the scale drawing above to show the position of Upton.

(An additional diagram, if required, can be found on *Page 35*)

3

[End of Paper 1]

ADDITIONAL SPACE FOR ANSWERS

Additional diagram for Question 7a)

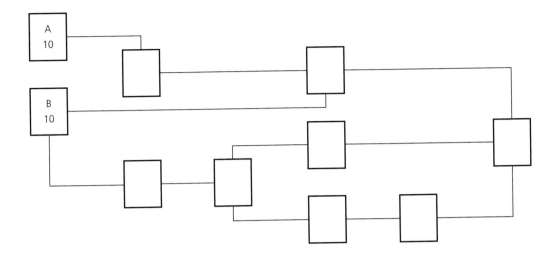

Additional diagram for Question 10b)

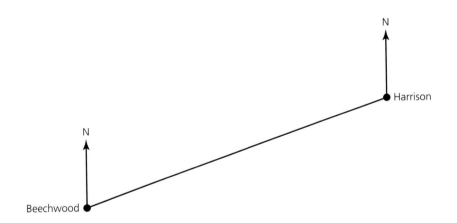

B

Paper 2 (calculator)

MARKS

1   Diane puts £5000 into a savings account with a rate of interest of 3·2% per annum.

At the end of each year, after the interest has been added, she withdraws £400.

How much will Diane have in the account at the end of the second year?

4

2 John and Steven are playing snooker. They play six games.

Shown below are the number of points John scored in each game.

39   22   54   45   43   46

a) Calculate:

   (i) the mean score

   (ii) the standard deviation, correct to one decimal place.

b) Steven's mean score and standard deviation were 44 points and 8·3 points respectively.

Make two valid comparisons between the number of points scored by Steven and John.

1

3

2

3 Emma Gould works in an insurance office.

Her salary is £28 200 per annum and she is paid monthly.

Her payslip for April 2016 is shown below.

There are some missing entries.

Name: E. Gould		Pay Period: 1/4/16 to 30/4/16	
Basic Pay £2350·00	**Overtime** £0·00	**Bonus** £0·00	**Gross Pay** £2350·00
Income Tax £	**National Insurance** £	**Pension** £142·00	**Total Deductions** £
			Net Pay £

a) Emma's personal allowance is £10 500 and she pays tax at the basic rate of 20%.

Calculate how much income tax she paid in April 2016.

3

b) Emma's National Insurance contribution is 12% on annual earnings over £8060.

She also pays £142 per month into her pension.

Calculate Emma's net pay in April 2016.

5

4   The distribution of the population in Caton village in 1920 is shown in the table and the pie chart below.

Population 1920

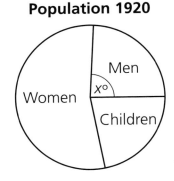

Population 1920	
Men	261
Women	582
Children	237
Total	1080

a)   **Calculate** the size of the angle marked $x°$ in the pie chart.

2

b)   By 1990 the population of Caton village had increased to 2133.
Express the increase as a percentage of the population in 1920.

2

c)   The pie charts below show the distribution of the population in Caton village in 1920 and 1990.

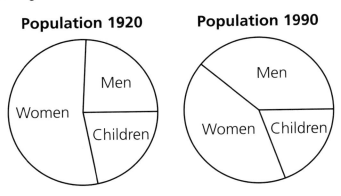

Compare the distribution of the population in Caton village in these two years.

2

5 Gillian went on holiday to the United States and Canada.

She flew to New York where she stayed in a hotel for 6 nights. She then flew from New York to Toronto in Canada where she stayed at a friend's house for a week before flying home to Scotland.

Her flights cost £780 in total. Her hotel in New York cost US$160 per night plus 15% tax.

Currency	Exchange rate
US Dollar	£1 = US$1·54
Canadian Dollar	£1 = C$2·04

a) Calculate the total cost of her flights and hotel in pounds sterling.

3

b) Gillian changed £1900 into US Dollars for the holiday.
She spent US$2000 while in New York and then changed all her remaining US Dollars in to Canadian Dollars before flying to Toronto.
How many Canadian Dollars did she receive?

3

c) The time in Toronto is 5 hours behind the time in Scotland.
When it is noon in Toronto it is 5 p.m. in Scotland.
Gillian's flight home leaves Toronto at 1855 local time and arrives in Edinburgh at 0645 local time the next morning. The distance of the flight is 3320 miles.
Calculate the average speed of the flight.
Give your answer correct to the nearest mile per hour.

3

6 A cable car runs between station A and station B as shown in the diagram.

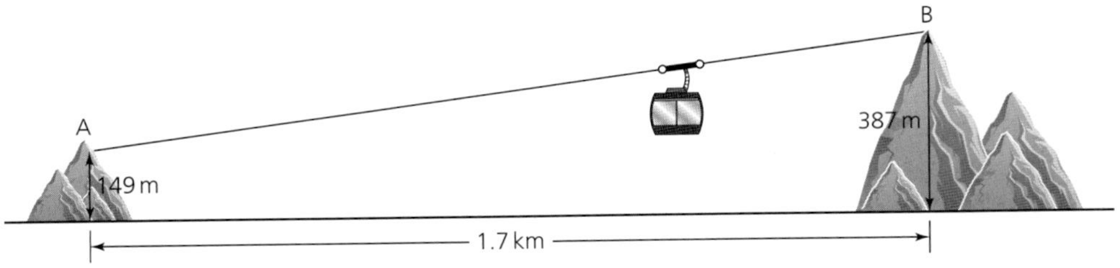

- The altitude of station A is 149 metres.
- The altitude of station B is 387 metres.
- The horizontal distance from station A to station B is 1·7 kilometres.

a) Calculate the gradient of the cable linking station A to station B.
Give your answer as a decimal.

2

b) The cable car runs at an average speed of 5 metres per second.
How long does it take to travel from station A to station B?
Give your answer in minutes and seconds to the nearest second.

6

c) The cable car:
- operates from 7 a.m. to 10 p.m. each day
- completes each round trip, including waiting times, in 18 minutes
- carries a maximum of 8 people.

Calculate the maximum number of people that the cable car can carry in a day.

1

7 a) Sally is going to make 4 litres of fruit punch for a party.
She is going to mix apple juice and mango juice in the ratio 3 : 2.
How much mango juice will she need to make the punch?

2

b) The supermarket sells apple juice and mango juice in 1 litre, 1·5 litre
and 2 litre cartons.
The prices of the cartons are £1·20, £1·80 and £2·30 respectively.

Sally wants to spend the minimum possible on buying enough apple
juice and mango juice to make the punch.
How many cartons of each size of apple juice and of mango juice should
Sally buy and what will this cost her?

2

c) The supermarket has the following offer on cartons of fruit juice.

5 for the price of 4

Cheapest carton free

Explain how this offer could save Sally money.

2

d) Sally is going to make the punch in a hemispherical bowl with diameter 24 centimetres.

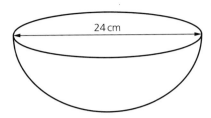

Will one bowl be big enough to hold 4 litres of punch?
Justify your answer.

3

e) At the party, Sally will serve the punch in conical glasses with diameter 7 centimetres and height 10 centimetres.

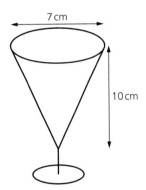

Each glass will be filled up to one centimetre from the top.
There are going to be twelve people at the party.
How many of these glasses of punch can each person have?

4

[End of Paper 2]

[END OF PRACTICE PAPER B]

ADDITIONAL SPACE FOR ANSWERS

National 5 Lifeskills Maths

National 5
Lifeskills Maths

Formulae list

Circumference of a circle: $C = \pi d$

Area of a circle: $A = \pi r^2$

Theorem of Pythagoras: 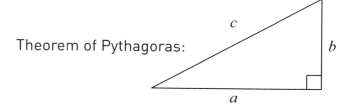 $a^2 + b^2 = c^2$

Volume of a cylinder: $V = \pi r^2 h$

Volume of a prism: $V = Ah$

Volume of a cone: $V = \frac{1}{3}\pi r^2 h$

Volume of a sphere: $V = \frac{4}{3}\pi r^3$

Standard deviation: $s = \sqrt{\dfrac{\Sigma(x - \bar{x})^2}{n-1}} = \sqrt{\dfrac{\Sigma x^2 - (\Sigma x)^2 / n}{n-1}}$, where n is the sample size.

Gradient: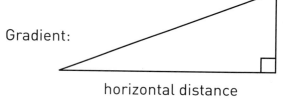

$$\text{gradient} = \frac{\text{vertical height}}{\text{horizontal distance}}$$

Paper 1 (non-calculator)

Total marks: 35

Attempt ALL questions.

You may NOT use a calculator.

Full credit will be given only to solutions which contain appropriate working.

State the units for your answer where appropriate.

Write your answers in the spaces provided in this booklet. Additional space for answers is provided at the end of this booklet. If you use this space you must clearly identify the question number you are attempting.

Use **blue** or **black** ink.

MARKS

1. Jim is going to lay paving slabs to form a garden path.

   The slabs are available in two lengths – 750 mm and 900 mm.

   Both types of slab are the same width.

   He would need 18 of the 750 mm slabs to form the path.

   How many of the 900 mm slabs would he need to form the path?   2

2. The average number of hours of sunshine per day in September last year in Edinburgh was 6.88 ± 0.005.

   Calculate the minimum number of hours of sunshine for the whole of September last year in Edinburgh.   3

3 Lindsay is flying from Edinburgh to Sydney with a short stopover in Doha.

She leaves Edinburgh at 1730 local time on Thursday 1 September.

The flight from Edinburgh to Doha takes 7 hours 20 minutes.

She has a stopover in Doha for 4 hours 30 minutes.

The flight from Doha to Sydney takes 15 hours 50 minutes.

Local time in Sydney is 11 hours ahead of local time in Edinburgh.

What is the date and local time when Lindsay arrives in Sydney?

MARKS

2

4 Every Tuesday for nine weeks the percentage cloud cover and the amount of rainfall (in millimetres) were recorded by a group of students.

The results are shown in the table below.

Cloud cover (%)	50	10	60	86	5	32	74	48	26
Rainfall (mm)	48	24	52	84	10	30	68	54	28

a) Plot this information on a scattergraph.

(An additional graph grid, if required, can be found on *Page 54*)

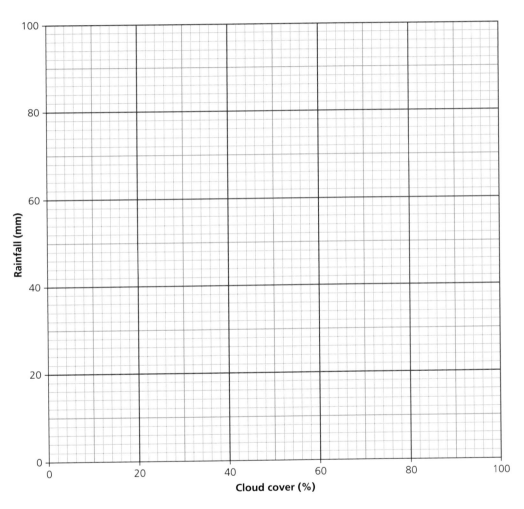

b) Draw a line of best fit on your scattergraph.

c) Use your line of best fit to estimate the amount of rainfall if there is 78% cloud cover.

2

1

1

C

5 Joan earns £8·60 per hour working in an office.

   In a typical month:

   - she works 150 hours
   - her net pay is $\frac{5}{6}$ of her gross pay
   - her outgoings are £995.

   How much money does she have left in a typical month after her outgoings have been paid?

3

6 Jeff is going to make some jam.

   He has 800 grams of sugar and 700 grams of fruit.

   The ratio of sugar to fruit in the jam **must be** 5 : 4.

   Does he have enough sugar and fruit to make 1·5 kilograms of the jam?

   Justify your answer.

3

7 Rose and Jim are booking a flight from Edinburgh to Amsterdam.

The price of the flight is £97·80 per person.

It costs an additional £28 for each piece of luggage booked into the plane's hold.

There is a $2\frac{1}{2}$% surcharge if the booking is paid by credit card.

How much would Rose and Jim pay in total for their flight to Amsterdam if they booked one piece of luggage between them into the hold and paid by credit card?

3

8 The birth weights (in kilograms) of the babies born in a hospital one year are shown in the boxplots below.

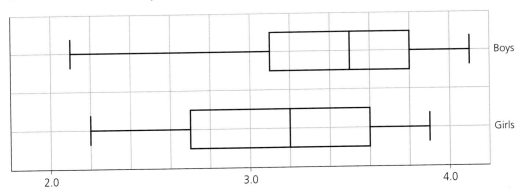

a) Write down the baby girls' median weight.

1

b) Calculate the baby boys' interquartile range.

2

c) Make two valid comparisons between the weights of the baby boys and girls.

MARKS

2

d) There were 260 baby boys born in the hospital in the year. Calculate how many of them weighed 3·8 kg or more at birth.

2

9 A concrete ramp is to be built.

The ramp is in the shape of a cuboid and a triangular prism with dimensions as shown.

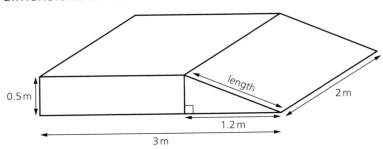

a) Calculate the length of the sloping edge of the ramp.

3

b) For safety reasons the gradient of the ramp should be less than 0·5.
Does the ramp meet this requirement?
Justify your answer.

2

c) Calculate the volume of concrete required to build the ramp.

3

[End of Paper 1]

ADDITIONAL SPACE FOR ANSWERS

Additional graph grid for Question 4a)

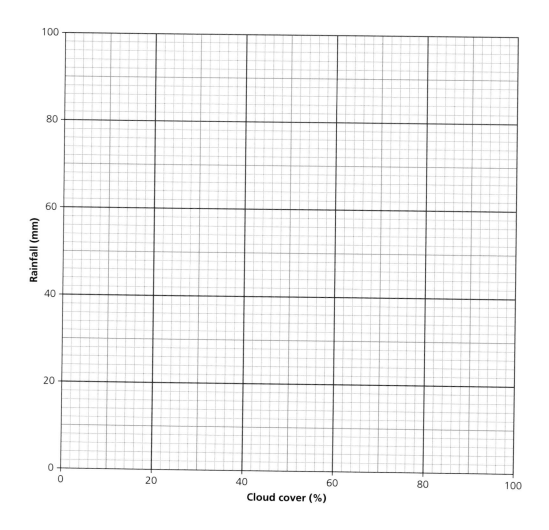

ADDITIONAL SPACE FOR ANSWERS

Paper 2 (calculator)

Total marks: 55

Attempt ALL questions.

You may use a calculator.

Full credit will be given only to solutions which contain appropriate working.

State the units for your answer where appropriate.

Write your answers clearly in the spaces provided in this booklet. Additional space for answers is provided at the end of this booklet. If you use this space you must clearly identify the question number you are attempting.

Use **blue** or **black** ink.

MARKS

1 The length of one lap of this athletics track is 400 metres.

   a) An athlete runs $3\frac{3}{4}$ laps of the track in 3 minutes 54·3 seconds.
Calculate the athlete's average speed in **metres per second**.

       3

   b) The straights on the track are 90 metres long and the bends are semi-circles.

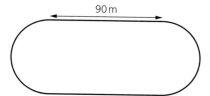

90 m

Calculate the diameter of the bends.

       3

2 Rebecca wants to buy a new television priced at £930 from the TV Store.

a) The Store offers her a finance package to pay for the television.
The deposit is 20% of the cash price, followed by 12 payments of £70.
Find the total to be paid for the television using the finance package.

3

b) Express the extra amount to be paid for the television using the finance package as a percentage of the cash price.
Give your answer correct to three significant figures.

3

c) Rebecca considers taking out a loan of £930 to pay for the television.
Simple interest will be charged at 11·2% per annum on the amount borrowed and she will repay the loan in equal monthly payments over one year.
Calculate the amount of each monthly payment.

3

3 The diagram below shows a plan of a deck floor on a cruise ship.

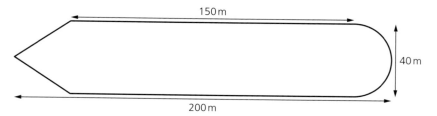

150 m

40 m

200 m

a) A scale drawing of this deck floor is made using a scale of 1:800.
Calculate the overall length of the deck floor **on the scale drawing**.
Give your answer in centimetres.

2

b) The deck floor consists of a triangle, a rectangle and a semi-circle.
Calculate the area of the deck floor.

4

c) The wooden parts of the deck floor are to be varnished.
- 75% of the deck floor is wooden.
- 1 litre of varnish covers an area of 15 m².
- Varnish is supplied in 20 litre tins.

How many 20 litre tins are needed to give the wooden parts of the deck
floor one coat of varnish?

3

4 Before travelling to Spain the Browns changed some pounds sterling to euros.

The exchange rate was £1 = Ð1·3293.

a) The bill for their meal one evening is Ð110.
The Browns pay for the meal in cash.
How much does the meal cost in pounds sterling?

1

b) The Browns could have paid for their meal by credit or debit card.
When a card is used to pay for goods and services abroad:
- You may be charged a transaction fee (a percentage of the bill).
- You may be charged a purchase fee.
- The exchange rate is different from that for changing currency.

The table below shows the exchange rate, transaction fee and purchase fee which apply to the Browns' credit and debit cards.

	Credit card	Debit card
Exchange rate	£1 = €1·3918	£1 = €1·3889
Transaction fee	2·95%	2·75%
Purchase fee	nil	£1·50

By which of the three methods of payment – cash, credit card or debit card – does the Browns' meal cost least in pounds sterling?
Show all working to justify your answer.

5

5 A farmer makes a rough sketch of one of his fields. He marks in the lengths of the four sides and the size of one of the angles as shown.

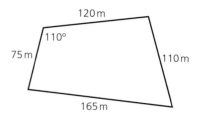

a) Using a suitable scale, make a scale drawing of the field.

3

b) The farmer is going to construct a post and rail fence around the field.

A fencing supplier gives him the following information to help him calculate the materials that he will need.

- Allow 4 m for the gate (including the gateposts).
- Allow one post for every 2 m of fence, plus one for each corner of the field.
- Allow three rails for every 4 m of fence.
- Allow 1 kg of nails for every 15 m of fence.

The prices of the materials are shown in the table below.

Item	Price (excluding VAT)
Gate (including gateposts and other fixings)	£380
Posts	£10 each
Rails	£8 each
Nails	£4·25 per kg

Calculate the cost (**including VAT at 20%**) of the materials that the farmer will need.

6

6 The temperatures, in degrees Celsius, at noon for the first ten days in November in Wilmington were:

13   11   4   2   −2   −3   −3   −1   0   −1

a) Calculate:

(i) the mean temperature

MARKS

1

(ii) the standard deviation, correct to one decimal place.

3

b) Calculate:

(i) the median temperature

1

(ii) the interquartile range.

2

c) Which of the two averages – the mean or the median – is more representative of the data?

Give a reason for your answer.

d) For the last ten days in November the mean temperature at noon in Wilmington was $5\,°C$ and the standard deviation was $3.2\,°C$.

Make two valid comparisons between the temperatures at noon in Wilmington for the first ten days and the last ten days in November.

7 A storage barn is prism-shaped, as shown below.

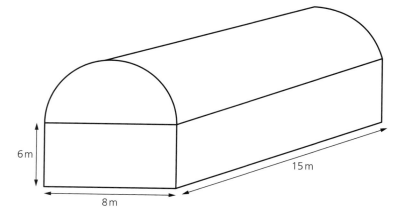

The cross-section of the storage barn consists of a rectangle and a semi-circle with dimensions as shown.

a) Find the volume of the storage barn.
Give your answer to the nearest cubic metre.

3

b) A prism-shaped extension to the barn, as shown below, is to be built.

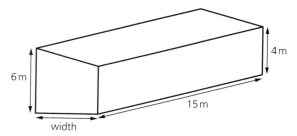

The cross-section of the extension consists of a rectangle and right-angled triangle.
The extension is planned to increase the volume by 250 cubic metres.
Find the width of the extension.
Give your answer correct to one decimal place.

3

[End of Paper 2]

[END OF PRACTICE PAPER C]

ADDITIONAL SPACE FOR ANSWERS

National 5
Lifeskills Maths

Practice Paper A

Paper 1 (non-calculator)

Question			Working	Mark		Note	Hint	HTP
1			$1700 \times 30p$	✓		Know how to calculate value	1·7 kg = 1700 g Remember the unit (£).	Ch3.3
			= £510	✓	2	Calculate value		
2			2253 to 0611= 7 h 18 min	✓		Calculate journey time	18 min = 18/60 h = 0·3 h Remember the unit (km).	
			$120 \times 7{\cdot}3$	✓		Know how to calculate distance		
			= 876 km	✓	3	Calculate distance		
3	a)			✓		Plot 3 points correctly	Horizontal scale: 2 squares to 1 unit	
				✓		Plot all 10 points correctly	Vertical scale: 1 square to 1 °C	Ch1.9
					2			
	b)		See above	✓		Draw line of best fit	The line should go roughly through the middle of all the points on the graph.	Ch1.9
					1			
	c)		9 °C	✓		Find temperature	The answer should be consistent with your line.	Ch1.9
					1			
4	a)		limits = 4·25 and 4·35	✓		Use lower and upper limits	Lower limit = 4·3 − 0·5 = 4·25	Ch2.7 and Ch1.6
			17 bolts within limits	✓		Find number of bolts within limits	Upper limit = 4·3 + 0·5 = 4·35	
			probability = $\dfrac{17}{20}$	✓	3	State probability		
	b)		$\dfrac{17}{20} \times 10\,000$	✓		Know how to calculate number of bolts	$10\,000 \div 20 \times 17$ = 500×17 = $100 \times 5 \times 17$	
			= 8500	✓	2	Calculate number of bolts	= $100 \times 85 = 8500$	

Question		Working	Mark	Note	Hint	HTP
5	a)	✓ ✓	2	Task letters in correct boxes Times in correct boxes		Ch2.5
	b)	A→B→C→E→G→H→I =19 days Yes, it will take 19 days and there are 20 working days in four weeks. ✓ ✓	2	Calculate total time Conclusion and valid reason	F can be carried out at same time as E. D → J can be carried out at same time as E → G → H → I and takes four days less to complete.	Ch2.5
6		700 ÷ 35 = 20 20 × 4·55 = 91 91 × £1·10 = £100·10 ✓ ✓ ✓	3	Calculate number of gallons Calculate number of litres Calculate cost	700 ÷ 35 = 700 ÷ 7 ÷ 5 = 100 ÷ 5 = 20 20 × 4·55 = 10 × 2 × 4·55 = 10 × 9·1 = 91 91 × 1·1 = 91 × 1 + 91 × 0·1 = 91 + 9·1 = 100·1 Remember the unit (£).	
7	a)	$\dfrac{5}{14}$ ✓	1	Find gradient	gradient = $\dfrac{\text{vertical}}{\text{horizontal}}$ $= \dfrac{12 - 7}{14}$	Ch2.8
	b)	$\dfrac{3}{8}$ $\dfrac{3}{8} = \dfrac{21}{56}$ $\dfrac{5}{14} = \dfrac{20}{56}$ Yes, as $\dfrac{21}{56} > \dfrac{20}{56}$ ✓ ✓ ✓	3	Find gradient of roof B Find common denominator Conclusion and reason	The least common multiple of 8 and 14 is the common denominator. e.g. multiples of 8: ... 32, 40, 48, 56, 64 ... multiples of 14: ... 28, 42, 56, 70 ...	Ch2.8
8		14 000 × 0·8 14 000 × 0·8 × 0·8 × 0·8 = 7168 14 000 × 0·8 × 0·8 × 0·8 × 0·8 = 5734·40 ⇒ 4 years ✓ ✓ ✓ ✓	4	Know how to decrease 14 000 by 20% Know how to decrease 14 000 by 20% each year for 3 years Calculate value after 3 years Calculate value after 4 years and state conclusion	100% – 20% = 80% = 0·8 Decreasing by 20% per annum for 3 years is not equal to a decrease of 3 × 20%. Remember the unit (years).	Ch1.5

Question	Working	Mark	Note	Hint	HTP
9	$d^2 = 6^2 + 8^2$	✓	Start to calculate base diagonal	Look for right-angled triangles to apply Pythagoras' Theorem.	Ch2.11 and Ch2.10
	$d = 10$	✓	Calculate base diagonal		
	$h^2 = 13^2 - 5^2$	✓	Start to calculate pyramid height		
	$h = 12$	✓	Calculate pyramid height		
	$V = \frac{1}{3} \times (6 \times 8) \times 12$	✓	Correct substitution into $\frac{1}{3}Ah$	Remember the unit (cm³).	
	$= 192 \text{ cm}^3$	✓ 6	Calculate volume		

Paper 2 (calculator)

Question			Working	Mark		Note	Hint	HTP
1	a)		43 800 – 10 740 = 33 060	✓		Know how to calculate taxable income	20% = 0·2, 40% = 0·4	Ch1.2
			0·2 × 31 875 = 6375	✓		Know how to calculate basic annual tax		
			0·4 × (33 060 – 31 875) = 474	✓		Know how to calculate annual tax at higher rate	Remember the unit (£).	
			6375 + 474 = £6849	✓	4	Calculate annual tax		
	b)		6849 ÷ 12 = 570·75	✓		Calculate monthly tax		Ch1.2
			570·75 + 343·20 + 273·75 = 1187·70	✓		Calculate monthly deductions	Remember the unit (£) and the final 0; 2462·3 is not enough.	
			43 800 ÷ 12 – 1187·70 = £2462·30	✓	3	Calculate monthly net pay		
2	a)		$\pi \times 4·1^2 \times 10 = 528·10$	✓		Calculate volume of can	Remember the unit (cm³). If $\pi = 3.14$ is used then volume of can = 527.834 leading to an answer of 501cm³.	p65, Example 9 p59, Example 1
			0·95 × 528·1= 501·69...	✓		Calculate volume of cola		
			= 502 cm³	✓	3	Round to 3 significant figures		
	b)		(35 ÷ 8·2) × (35 ÷ 8·2) × (25 ÷10) → 4 × 4 × 2 = 32	✓		Calculate and justify how many cans can be fitted into mini fridge	You must show that 36 cans is the maximum by considering the other possibility.	Ch2.4
			(35 ÷ 10) × (35 ÷ 8·2) × (25 ÷ 8·2) → 3 × 4 × 3 = 36 so maximum = 36 cans	✓	2	Calculate and justify the maximum number of cans that can be fitted into mini fridge		
	c)		35 × 35 × 25 = 30 625 36 × 502 = 18 072	✓		Calculate volume of mini fridge and volume of cans	% occupied = volume of cans ÷ volume of mini fridge × 100	Ch2.10 p63, Example 4
			$\dfrac{18 072}{30 625} \times 100$	✓		Know how to calculate percentage		
			= 59%	✓	3	Calculate percentage		
3			20 × 32·71 = 654·20	✓		Convert £20 into CZK	Convert £→CZK and €→£→CZK	Ch1.4
			100 ÷ 1·38 × 32·71 = 2370·29	✓		Convert €100 into CZK correct to 2 decimal places		
			(654·20 + 2370·29) – 3000 = CZK24·49	✓	3	Calculate change correct to 2 decimal places.	Remember the unit (CZK).	

Question		Working	Mark		Note	Hint	HTP
4	a)	Boisdale shown on bearing of (060 ± 2)° from Ardpoint Cairnross shown on bearing of (155 ± 2)° from Boisdale e.g. 1 cm : 5 km AB = (8 ± 0·2) cm BC = (11 ± 0·2) cm 	✓ ✓ ✓ 3		One bearing correct Second bearing correct Lengths consistent with stated scale	You must state the scale that you have chosen to use. Bearings are measured clockwise from North.	Ch2.3
	b)	e.g. 13 × 5 = 65 km 297°	✓ ✓ 2		Calculate distance Find bearing	Remember the units (km and °).	Ch2.3
	c)	0940→1730 – 30 min = 7 h 20 min (40 + 55 + 65) ÷ 7·33... = 21·8 = 22 km/h	✓ ✓ ✓ 3		Calculate travelling time Know how to calculate average speed Calculate average speed correct to nearest km/h	7 h 20 min = 7·33...h; do not round it to 7·3 h. Remember the unit (km/h).	
5	a)	6 × 12·50 + 6 × 22·50 = 210 210 + 49·95 + 12 × 17·50 = £469·95	✓ ✓ 2		Calculate package fee Calculate total cost	Remember the unit (£).	Ch1.3
	b)	31·75 + 12 × (20 + 16·99) = 475·63 12 × 0·5 × 27 = 162 55·95 + 162 + 12 × 17·99 = 433·83 Scotcall offers the best deal	✓ ✓ ✓ ✓ 4		Calculate Teleview total cost Calculate Scotcall package fee Calculate Scotcall total cost Conclusion	Remember to state a conclusion.	Ch1.3
	c)	Teleview because its package fee and line rental are both cheaper than those of the other companies.	✓ 1		Conclusion and valid reason	Remember to give a valid reason for your answer.	Ch1.3

Question			Working	Mark		Note	Hint	HTP
6	a)		$0.6 \times (2.4 + 2.1) = 2.7$	✓		Calculate area of wood	Remember the unit (£).	Ch2.9
			$2.7 \times 49.99 = £134.97$	✓		Calculate cost of wood to the nearest penny		
					2			
	b)		$2 \times (\frac{1}{2} \times 0.6 \times 0.6)$	✓		Know how to calculate area of the triangular cut-offs	Remember the unit (m²).	Ch2.9
			$0.6^2 - \frac{1}{4} \times \pi \times 0.6^2$	✓		Know how to calculate area of the curved cut-off		
			$0.36 + 0.077... = 0.44\,m^2$	✓		Calculate the total area of the cut-offs and round to 2 decimal places		
					3			
	c)		$\frac{1}{4} \times \pi \times 1.2$ $= 0.94$	✓		Know how to calculate length of arc AB	Remember the unit (m).	Ch2.9
			BC = 1.2, CD = 1.5	✓		Calculate length of BC or CD		
			$0.94 + 1.2 + 1.5 = 3.64\,m$	✓		Calculate length of edging strip		
					3			
7	a)	(i)	27	✓		Correct median		Ch1.7
			23 and 32	✓	2	Correct quartiles		
		(ii)	18 23 27 32 40	✓		Endpoints at 18 and 40	Draw your boxplot to a suitable scale and label all five points.	Ch1.7
				✓	2	Correct box showing 23, 27 and 32		
	b)		$\frac{4}{17}$	✓	1	State probability		Ch3.8
	c)		$P(2^{nd}\ team) = \frac{1}{4}$	✓		Interpret boxplot	Each section of the boxplot represents $\frac{1}{4}$ of the team.	Ch3.8
			$\frac{1}{4} = 0.25, \frac{4}{17} = 0.235...$	✓		Compare probabilities		
			2nd team since 0.25 > 0.235...	✓		Conclusion and reason		
					3			
	d)	(i)	(179 + 187 + 193 + 184 + 185 + 182) ÷ 6 = 185 cm	✓	1	Calculate mean	Remember the unit (cm).	Ch1.8

Question		Working	Mark		Note	Hint	HTP
	(ii)	**Method 1**				All of the entries in the $(x - \bar{x})^2$ column should be positive.	

Method 1

x	$x - \bar{x}$	$(x - \bar{x})^2$
179	−6	36
187	2	4
193	8	64
184	−1	1
185	0	0
182	−3	9
	$\sum(x - \bar{x})^2 = 114$	

✓   Calculate $(x - \bar{x})^2$ i.e. 36, 4, 64, 1, 0 and 9

When using a calculator to square a negative number, e.g. −6, enter $(-6)^2$ to obtain an answer of 36.

$$s = \sqrt{\frac{114}{5}}$$

✓   Substitute correctly into standard deviation formula

Remember the unit (cm).

$$= 4 \cdot 8 \, \text{cm}$$

✓   Calculate standard deviation

Method 2

Ch1.8

x	x^2
179	32 041
187	34 969
193	37 249
184	33 856
185	34 225
182	33 124
$\sum x = 1110$	$\sum x^2 = 205 464$

✓   Calculate $\sum x$ and $\sum x^2$ i.e. 1110 and 205 464

$$s = \sqrt{\frac{205 464 - \dfrac{1110^2}{6}}{5}}$$

✓   Substitute correctly into standard deviation formula

$$= 4 \cdot 8 \, \text{cm}$$

✓   Calculate standard deviation

Mark: 3

	e)	On average the defenders are taller.	✓		Valid comment regarding the mean	Comments must be related to the context of the question and show an understanding that mean is an average and standard deviation is a measure of spread. Simply stating that the mean is higher and the standard deviation is lower gains 0 marks.	Ch1.8
		The defenders' heights are more consistent.	✓		Valid comment regarding the standard deviation		
				2			

Practice Paper B

Paper 1 (non-calculator)

Question			Working	Mark		Note	Hint	HTP
1			148 Yes, 148 lies between the acceptable limits of 147 and 153	✓ ✓ 2		Read scale Conclusion and valid reason	lower limit = 150 − 3 = 147 upper limit = 150 + 3 = 153	Ch2.7
2			$\dfrac{36}{90}$ $\dfrac{2}{5}$	✓ ✓ 2		Find probability Express in simplest form		Ch1.6
3			$\dfrac{2.70}{360} \times 1000$ = £7·50	✓ ✓ 2		Know how to calculate price per kg Calculate price per kg	Remember the unit (£) and the final 0; 7·5 is not enough.	Ch2.1
4			15% of 26·60 = 3·99 10 × 3·99 = 39·90 ⇒ 11 × 3·99 > 40 ⇒ 11 return tickets	✓ ✓ 2		Calculate discount Calculate number of return tickets	15% of 26·60 = 10% of 26·60 + 5% of 26·60 = 2·66 + 1·33 = 3·99 11 × 3·99 = 10 × 3·99 + 1 × 3·99 = 39·9 + 3·99 = 43·98	
5			$\dfrac{3}{5}+\dfrac{3}{5}+\dfrac{3}{5}+\dfrac{3}{5}+\dfrac{3}{5}$ $=\dfrac{15}{5}=3$ 5 loaves can be baked with 3 bags, so 10 loaves can be baked with 6 bags.	✓ ✓ 2		Start valid strategy Calculate number of loaves	Alternative method $6 \div \dfrac{3}{5} = 6 \times \dfrac{5}{3} = \dfrac{30}{3}$ = 10	p66, Example 12
6			$\dfrac{1}{4} \times 3{\cdot}14 \times 60^2$ or $\dfrac{1}{4} \times 3{\cdot}14 \times 40^2$ $\dfrac{1}{4} \times 3{\cdot}14 \times 60^2 - \dfrac{1}{4} \times 3{\cdot}14 \times 40^2$ = 2826 − 1256 = 1570 m²	✓ ✓ ✓ 3		Correct substitution into $\dfrac{1}{4} \times 3{\cdot}14 \times r^2$ for either sector of circle Know to subtract smaller sector from larger sector Calculate area	$\dfrac{1}{4} \times 3{\cdot}14 \times 3600$ $=\dfrac{1}{4} \times 3600 \times 3{\cdot}14$ = 900 × 3·14 = 9 × 100 × 3·14 = 9 × 314 = 2826 Remember the unit (m²).	Ch2.9

Question			Working	Mark		Note	Hint	HTP
7	a)			✓ ✓ **2**		Task letters in correct boxes Times in correct boxes		Ch2.5
	b)		A→C→D→J =130 minutes 7.30 p.m. – 2 h 10 min = 5.20 p.m.	✓ ✓ **2**		Calculate total time taken Calculate starting time	B can be carried out at same time as A. E→ F→G or E→ F→H→I can be carried out at same time as C→D but take less time to complete.	Ch2.5
8	a)		23 + 16·95 + 16·95 = 56·90 34·50 56·90 – 34·50 = £22·40	✓ ✓ ✓ **3**		Calculate cost of sending parcels individually Find cost of sending as one parcel Calculate saving	Remember the unit (£) and the final 0; 22.4 is not enough.	Ch3.6
	b)		<table><tr><th>Parcel</th><th>Weight of individual parcels (kg)</th><th>Total weight of parcel (kg)</th></tr><tr><td>1</td><td>14 + 5</td><td>19</td></tr><tr><td>2</td><td>13 + 7</td><td>20</td></tr><tr><td>3</td><td>12 + 8</td><td>20</td></tr><tr><td>4</td><td>11 + 9</td><td>20</td></tr><tr><td>5</td><td>7 + 5 + 4 + 3</td><td>19</td></tr></table>	✓ ✓ **2**		Three rows of table correct Other two rows of table correct		Ch2.4
9	a)	(i)	18 hours 15 and 24 24 – 15 = 9 hours	✓ ✓ ✓ **3**		Correct median Correct quartiles Correct interquartile range		Ch1.7

Question			Working	Mark		Note	Hint	HTP
	a)	(ii)	11 15 18 24 31	✓		Endpoints at 11 and 31	Draw your boxplot to a suitable scale and label all five points.	Ch1.7
				✓	2	Correct box showing 15, 18 and 24		
	b)		On average the number of hours of sunshine was more in Portree. The number of hours of sunshine was more consistent in Portree.	✓		Valid comment regarding the median	Comments must be related to the context of the question and show an understanding that median is an average and IQR is a measure of spread. Simply stating that the median is higher and the IQR is lower gains 0 marks.	Ch1.8
				✓	2	Valid comment regarding the spread		
10	a)		8·5 × 40 = 340 km 070°	✓		Know how to calculate distance	8·5 × 40 = 8·5 × 10 × 4 = 85 × 4 = 340 Remember the units (km and °).	Ch2.3
				✓		Calculate distance		
				✓	3	Find bearing		
	b)			✓		One bearing correct	Bearings are measured clockwise from North.	Ch2.3
				✓		Second bearing correct		
				✓	3	Intersection of two bearings shown		

Paper 2 (calculator)

Question			Working	Mark		Note	Hint	HTP
1			$5000 \times 0.032 = 160$	✓		Calculate interest in first year	$3.2\% = 0.032$	
			$5000 + 160 - 400 = 4760$	✓		Calculate amount at end of first year		
			$4760 \times 1.032 - 400$	✓		Know how to calculate amount at end of second year	$100\% + 3.2\% = 103.2\%$ $= 1.032$	Ch1.5
			$= £4512.32$	✓	**4**	Calculate amount at end of second year	Remember the unit (£).	
2	a)	(i)	$(39 + 22 + 54 + 45 + 43 + 46) \div 6 = 41.5$ points	✓	**1**	Calculate mean		Ch1.8
		(ii)	**Method 1** <table><tr><td>x</td><td>$x - \bar{x}$</td><td>$(x - \bar{x})^2$</td></tr><tr><td>39</td><td>−2.5</td><td>6.25</td></tr><tr><td>22</td><td>−19.5</td><td>380.25</td></tr><tr><td>54</td><td>12.5</td><td>156.25</td></tr><tr><td>45</td><td>3.5</td><td>12.25</td></tr><tr><td>43</td><td>1.5</td><td>2.25</td></tr><tr><td>46</td><td>4.5</td><td>20.25</td></tr><tr><td></td><td colspan="2">$\sum(x-\bar{x})^2 = 577.5$</td></tr></table> $s = \sqrt{\dfrac{577.5}{5}}$ $= 10.7$ points **Method 2** <table><tr><td>x</td><td>x^2</td></tr><tr><td>39</td><td>1521</td></tr><tr><td>22</td><td>484</td></tr><tr><td>54</td><td>2916</td></tr><tr><td>45</td><td>2025</td></tr><tr><td>43</td><td>1849</td></tr><tr><td>46</td><td>2116</td></tr><tr><td>$\sum x = 249$</td><td>$\sum x^2 = 10911$</td></tr></table> $s = \sqrt{\dfrac{10911 - \dfrac{249^2}{6}}{5}}$ $= 10.7$ points	✓ ✓ ✓ ✓ ✓ ✓	**3**	Calculate $(x - \bar{x})^2$ i.e. 6.25, 380.25, 156.25, 12.25, 2.25 and 20.25 Substitute correctly into standard deviation formula Calculate standard deviation Calculate $\sum x$ and $\sum x^2$ i.e. 249 and 10911 Substitute correctly into standard deviation formula Calculate standard deviation	All of the entries in the $(x - \bar{x})^2$ column should be positive. When using a calculator to square a negative number, e.g. −2.5, enter $(-2.5)^2$ to obtain an answer of 6.25.	Ch1.8

Question		Working	Mark	Note	Hint	HTP
	b)	On average Steven scored more points.	✓	Valid comment regarding the mean	Comments must be related to the context of the question and show an understanding that mean is an average and standard deviation is a measure of spread. Simply stating that the mean is higher and the standard deviation is lower gains 0 marks.	Ch1.8
		Steven's scores were more consistent.	✓	Valid comment regarding the standard deviation		
			2			
3	a)	28 200 − 10 500 = 17 700	✓	Calculate taxable income	20% = 0·2	
		0·2 × 17 700 = 3540	✓	Calculate annual tax	Remember the unit (£).	Ch1.2
		3540 ÷ 12 = £295	✓ 3	Calculate monthly tax		
	b)	28 200 − 8060 = 20 140	✓	Calculate income subject to NI contribution		
		0·12 × 20 140 = 2416·80	✓	Calculate annual NI contribution	12% = 0·12	
		2416·80 ÷ 12 = 201·40	✓	Calculate monthly NI contribution	Remember the unit (£) and the final 0; 1711·6 is not enough.	Ch1.2
		295 + 201·40 + 142 = 638·40	✓	Calculate total deductions		
		28 200 ÷ 12 − 638·40 = £1711·60	✓ 5	Calculate net pay		
4	a)	$\frac{261}{1080} \times 360°$	✓	Know how to calculate x°	Remember the unit (°).	
		= 87°	✓ 2	Calculate x°		Ch3.6
	b)	$\frac{(2133 - 1080)}{1080} \times 100$	✓	Know how to calculate percentage increase	% increase $= \frac{increase}{original\ value} \times 100$	p63, Example 4
		= 97·5%	✓ 2	Calculate percentage increase		
	c)	In 1990 the proportion of men had increased; the proportion of women had decreased; the proportion of children was about the same.	✓ ✓	One valid comparison / One other valid comparison	Comparisons are based on the relative sizes of the corresponding sectors in the pie charts.	Ch3.6
			2			
5	a)	6 × 160 × 1·15 = 1104	✓	Know how to calculate cost of hotel in dollars	100% + 15% = 115% = 1·15	
		1104 ÷ 1·54 = 716·88	✓	Know how to calculate cost of hotel in pounds	Cost should be given to nearest penny.	Ch1.4
		716·88 + 780 = £1496·88	✓ 3	Calculate total cost of hotel and flights in pounds	Remember the unit (£).	

Question			Working	Mark		Note	Hint	HTP
	b)		$1900 \times 1.54 = 2926$	✓		Convert £1900 into US$	Cost should be given to nearest cent. Remember the unit (C$).	Ch1.4
			$2926 - 2000 = 926$	✓		Calculate amount to be converted into C$		
			$926 \div 1.54 = £601.30$ $601.30 \times 2.04 = C\$1226.65$	✓	3	Convert remaining amount into C$		
	c)		$1855 \to 0645 - 5\,h$ $= 6\,h\,50\,min$	✓		Calculate flight time	$6\,h\,50\,min = 6.833...\,h$; do not round it to 6.8 h. Remember the unit (m.p.h.).	
			$3320 \div 6.833...$	✓		Know how to calculate average speed		
			$= 486\,m.p.h.$	✓	3	Calculate average speed to nearest m.p.h.		
6	a)		$\dfrac{238}{1700}$	✓		Find gradient	gradient = $\dfrac{\text{vertical}}{\text{horizontal}}$	Ch2.8
			$= 0.14$	✓	2	Express gradient as a decimal		
	b)		$AB^2 = 238^2 + 1700^2$	✓		Correct use of Pythagoras' Theorem		Ch2.11 and p.ix example
			$= 2\,946\,644$	✓		Calculate AB^2		
			$AB = 1716.57...$	✓		Calculate AB		
			$1716.57... \div 5$	✓		Know how to calculate time		
			$= 343.3...\,sec$	✓		Calculate time		
			$= 5\,min\,43\,sec$	✓	6	Convert time to minutes and seconds to nearest second		
	c)		$(15 \times 60) \div 18 \times 8 = 400$	✓	1	Calculate maximum number of people		
7	a)		$\dfrac{2}{5} \times 4$	✓		Know how to calculate amount of mango juice	apple : mango = 3 : 2 => $\dfrac{3}{5}$ apple, $\dfrac{2}{5}$ mango	p66, Example 13
			$= 1.6\,l$ or $1600\,ml$	✓	2	Calculate amount of mango juice		
	b)		e.g. Apple 1×2 litre, 1×1 litre; Mango 1×2 litre; cost = £5·80	✓		Calculate and justify cost of any combination that provides enough of each juice		Ch1.3
			Apple 1×1 litre, 1×1.5 litre; Mango 1×2 litre; cost = £5·30	✓	2	Calculate and justify optimal cost		
	c)		5×1 litre cartons costs £4·80	✓		Find cost		Ch1.3
			3×1 litre of apple juice and 2×1 litre of mango juice	✓	2	Explain combination of cartons		
	d)		$\dfrac{4}{3} \times \pi \times 12^3$	✓		Correct substitution into $\dfrac{4}{3}\pi r^3$	1 litre = 1000 ml = 1000 cm³	Ch2.10
			$\dfrac{4}{3} \times \pi \times 12^3 \div 2 = 3619.1...$	✓		Calculate volume of hemisphere		
			No, $3619\,ml < 4000\,ml$	✓	3	Conclusion and reason		

Question		Working	Mark	Note	Hint	HTP
	e)	$\frac{1}{3} \times \pi \times 3\cdot5^2 \times 9$	✓	Correct substitution into $\frac{1}{3}\pi r^2 h$	Alternative method: $115\cdot45... \times 12$	
		$= 115\cdot45...$			$= 1385\cdot44...$	
		$4000 \div 115\cdot45...$	✓	Know how to calculate number of glasses obtained from 4 litres	$4000 \div 1385\cdot44...$	
		$= 34\cdot64...$			$= 2\cdot88... => 2$ glasses	
		$34\cdot64... \div 12$	✓	Know how to calculate number of glasses for each person		Ch2.10
		$= 2\cdot88... \Rightarrow 2$ glasses	✓	Calculate number of complete glasses for each person		
			4			

Practice Paper C

Paper 1 (non-calculator)

Question		Working	Mark		Note	Hint	HTP
1		$750 \times 18 \div 900$ $= 15$	✓ ✓ **2**		Know how to calculate number of slabs Calculate number of slabs	$750 \times 18 \div 900$ $= 750 \times 2 \times 9 \div 900$ $= 1500 \times 9 \div 900$ $= 500 \div 9$ $= 15$	Ch2.1
2		$6{\cdot}88 - 0{\cdot}005 = 6{\cdot}875$ $6{\cdot}875 \times 30$ $= 206{\cdot}25$ hours	✓ ✓ ✓ **3**		Find minimum number of hours per day Know how to calculate minimum number of hours in September Calculate minimum number of hours in September	$6{\cdot}875 \times 30$ $= 6{\cdot}875 \times 10 \times 3$ $= 68{\cdot}75 \times 3$ $= 206{\cdot}25$	Ch2.7
3		$1730 + (7\,h\,20\,min + 4\,h\,30\,min +$ $15\,h\,50\,min) + 11\,h$ $= 1730 + 38\,h\,40\,min$ Saturday 3 September 0810	✓ ✓ **2**		Know how to calculate arrival time Calculate arrival date and time		Ch2.6
4	a)		✓ ✓ **2**		Plot 3 points correctly Plot all 9 points correctly	Horizontal scale: 1 square to 2% Vertical scale: 1 square to 2 mm	Ch1.9
	b)	See above	✓ **1**		Draw line of best fit	The line should go roughly through the middle of all the points on the graph.	Ch1.9
	c)	72 mm	✓ **1**		Find rainfall	The answer should be consistent with your line.	Ch1.9

Question		Working	Mark		Note	Hint	HTP
5		$8\cdot60 \times 150 = 1290$	✓		Calculate gross pay	Remember the unit (£).	Ch1.2 and Ch1.1
		$\frac{5}{6} \times 1290 = 1075$	✓		Calculate net pay		
		$1075 - 995 = £80$	✓	3	Calculate amount left		
6		$\frac{4}{9} \times 1500 = 666.6$	✓		Calculate required amount of fruit		p66, Example 13
		$\frac{5}{9} \times 1500 = 833.3$	✓		Calculate required amount of sugar		
		He does not have enough sugar; he only has 800g and he needs 833g. He has enough fruit; he has 700g and he needs 667g.	✓	3	Conclusion and valid reason		
7		$97\cdot80 \times 2 + 28 = 223\cdot60$	✓		Calculate cost before surcharge	10% of 223·60 is 22·36	
		$2\cdot5\%$ of $223\cdot60 = 5\cdot59$	✓		Calculate surcharge	=> 5% is 22·36 ÷ 2 = 11·18	
		$223\cdot60 + 5\cdot59 = £229\cdot19$	✓	3	Calculate total cost	=>2·5% is 11·18 ÷ 2 = 5·59 Remember the unit (£).	
8	a)	$3\cdot2$ kg	✓	1	Correct median	Remember the unit (kg).	Ch1.7
	b)	$3\cdot1$ and $3\cdot8$	✓		Correct quartiles	Remember the unit (kg).	Ch1.7
		$3\cdot8 - 3\cdot1 = 0\cdot7$ kg	✓	2	Calculate interquartile range		
	c)	On average the boys are heavier.	✓		Valid comment regarding the mean	Comments must be related to the context of the question and show an understanding that median is an average and IQR is a measure of spread. Simply stating that the median is higher and the IQR is lower gains 0 marks.	Ch1.8
		The boys' weights are more consistent.	✓	2	Valid comment regarding the interquartile range		
	d)	$\frac{1}{4}$ of 260	✓		Know that $\frac{1}{4}$ of the boys weighed 3·8 kg or more	Upper quartile = 3·8 kg => $\frac{1}{4}$ of the boys weighed 3·8 kg or more.	Ch1.8
		$= 65$	✓	2	Calculate $\frac{1}{4}$ of 260		

Question			Working	Mark		Note	Hint	HTP
9	a)		length^2 = 1·2^2 + 0·5^2	✓		Correct Pythagoras' statement		
			= 1·69	✓		Correct calculation of length^2	Remember the unit (m).	Ch2.11
			length = 1·3 m	✓	3	Calculate length of sloping edge		
	b)		$\frac{0·5}{1·2}$	✓		Correct gradient	gradient = $\frac{\text{vertical}}{\text{horizontal}}$	
			Yes, since $\frac{0·6}{1·2}$ = 0·5 and so $\frac{0·5}{1·2}$ < 0·5	✓	2	Conclusion and valid reason	Remember to give a valid reason for your answer.	Ch2.8
	c)		1·8 × 2 × 0·5 = 1·8	✓		Calculate volume of cuboid	solid = cuboid + triangular prism	
			$\frac{1}{2}$ × 1·2 × 2 × 0·5 = 0·6	✓		Calculate volume of triangular prism	Remember the unit (m^3).	Ch2.10
			1·8 + 0·6 = 2·4 m^3	✓	3	Calculate volume of concrete		

Paper 2 (calculator)

Question		Working	Mark		Note	Hint	HTP
1	a)	$3\frac{3}{4} \times 400 = 1500$ $1500 \div 234 \cdot 3$ $= 6 \cdot 4...\text{m/s}$	✓ ✓ ✓ **3**		Calculate distance Know how to calculate average speed Calculate average speed	$3\frac{3}{4} \times 400$ $= 3 \cdot 75 \times 400$ Remember the unit (m/s).	
	b)	$400 - 180 = 220$ $\pi d = 220$ $d = 220 \div \pi = 70\,\text{m}$	✓ ✓ ✓ **3**		Calculate total length of bends Correct substitution into circumference of circle formula Calculate diameter of bends	Remember the unit (m).	Ch2.9
2	a)	$0 \cdot 2 \times 930 = 186$ $12 \times 70 = 840$ $186 + 840 = £1026$	✓ ✓ ✓ **3**		Calculate deposit Calculate payments Calculate total cost	$20\% = 0 \cdot 2$ Remember the unit (£).	Ch1.5
	b)	$\dfrac{96}{930} \times 100$ $= 10 \cdot 32...$ $\Rightarrow 10 \cdot 3\%$	✓ ✓ ✓ **3**		Know how to calculate percentage Calculate percentage Round to 3 significant figures		p63, Example 4 p59, Example 1
	c)	$0 \cdot 112 \times 930 = 104 \cdot 16$ $930 + 104 \cdot 16 = 1034 \cdot 16$ $1034 \cdot 16 \div 12 = £86 \cdot 18$	✓ ✓ ✓ **3**		Calculate interest Calculate amount to be repaid Calculate monthly repayment	$11 \cdot 2\% = 0 \cdot 112$ Remember the unit (£).	Ch1.5
3	a)	$200\,\text{m} \div 800$ $= 0 \cdot 25\,\text{m}$ $= 25\,\text{cm}$	✓ ✓ **2**		Know how to calculate the length on the scale drawing Calculate the length on the scale drawing in centimetres	Remember the unit (cm).	Ch2.2
	b)	$\dfrac{1}{2} \times \pi \times 20^2$ $= 628$ $628 + 150 \times 40$ $= 6628$ $6628 + \dfrac{1}{2} \times 40 \times 30$ $= 7228\,\text{m}^2$	✓ ✓ ✓ ✓ **4**		Correct substitution into $\frac{1}{2}\pi r^2$ Correct substitution into lb and know to add to $\frac{1}{2}\pi r^2$ Correct substitution into $\frac{1}{2}bh$ and know to add to $\frac{1}{2}\pi r^2 + lb$ Calculate area of deck floor	Remember the unit (m²).	Ch2.9

Question		Working	Mark		Note	Hint	HTP
	c)	$0.75 \times 7228 = 5421$	✓		Calculate area to be varnished	75% = 0.75	
		$5421 \div 15 = 361.4$	✓		Calculate number of litres of varnish required		
		$361.4 \div 20 = 18.07$ $\Rightarrow$ 19 tins	✓	3	Calculate number of tins of varnish required		
4	a)	$110 \div 1.3293 = £82.750...$ $= £82.75$	✓	1	Convert cost into pounds	Remember the unit (£).	Ch1.4
	b)	Credit card $110 \times 1.0295 = €113.245$ $113.245 \div 1.3918 =$ $81.365...$ $\Rightarrow £81.37$	✓ ✓		Calculate total cost in euros with credit card Calculate total cost in pounds with credit card	100% + 2.95% = 102.95% = 1.0295	Ch1.5 and Ch1.4
		Debit card $110 \times 1.0275 = €113.025$ $113.025 \div 1.3889$ $= 81.377...$ $\Rightarrow 81.38 + 1.50 = £82.88$	✓ ✓		Calculate cost in euros with debit card including transaction fee Calculate total cost in pounds with debit card	100% + 2.75% = 102.75% = 1.0275 The conclusion must be supported by previous working.	
		Credit card is cheapest.	✓	5	Conclusion		
5	a)	e.g. for a scale of 1 cm to 10 m 7.5 ± 0.2 cm and 12 ± 0.2 cm $110° \pm 2°$ remaining sides 16.5 ± 0.2 cm and 11 ± 0.2 cm	✓ ✓ ✓		Draw 75 m and 120 m sides to chosen scale Draw angle of 110° correctly Complete scale drawing		Ch2.2
				3			
	b)	$120 + 110 + 165 + 75 - 4$ $= 466$	✓		Calculate length of fencing	100% + 20% = 120% = 1.2	
		$466 \div 2 + 4 = 237$	✓		Calculate number of posts	Remember the unit (£) and the final 0; 6823.2 is not enough.	
		$466 \div 4 \times 3 = 349.5 \Rightarrow$ 350	✓		Calculate number of rails		
		$466 \div 15 = 31.06... \Rightarrow 32$	✓		Calculate amount of nails		
		$380 + 237 \times 10 + 350 \times 8$ $+ 32 \times 4.25 = 5686$	✓		Calculate cost excluding VAT		
		$5686 \times 1.2 = £6823.20$	✓	6	Calculate cost including VAT		

Question			Working	Mark	Note	Hint	HTP
6	a)	(i)	$[13 + 11 + 4 + 2 + (-2) +$ $(-3) + (-3) + (-1) + 0 +$ $(-1)] \div 10 = 2\,°C$	✓	Calculate mean	Remember the unit (°C).	Ch1.8
				1			

(ii) Method 1

x	$x - \bar{x}$	$(x - \bar{x})^2$
13	11	121
11	9	81
4	2	4
2	0	0
−2	−4	16
−3	−5	25
−3	−5	25
−1	−3	9
0	−2	4
−1	−3	9
		$\sum(x - \bar{x})^2 = 294$

✓ — Calculate $(x - \bar{x})^2$ i.e. 121, 81, 4, 0, 16, 25, 25, 9, 4 and 9

Hint: All of the entries in the $(x - \bar{x})^2$ column should be positive.

When using a calculator to square a negative number, e.g. −4, enter $(-4)^2$ to obtain an answer of 16.

Remember the unit (°C).

$$s = \sqrt{\frac{294}{9}}$$

✓ — Substitute correctly into standard deviation formula

$$= 5\cdot7\,°C$$

✓ — Calculate standard deviation

Method 2

✓ — Calculate $\sum x$ and $\sum x^2$ i.e. 20 and 334

x	x^2
13	169
11	121
4	16
2	4
−2	4
−3	9
−3	9
−1	1
0	0
−1	1
$\sum x = 20$	$\sum x^2 = 334$

$$s = \sqrt{\frac{334 - \frac{20^2}{10}}{9}}$$

✓ — Substitute correctly into standard deviation formula

$$= 5\cdot7\,°C$$

✓ — Calculate standard deviation

| | **3** | |

HTP: Ch1.8

Question			Working	Mark		Note	Hint	HTP
	b)	(i)	−0.5 °C	✓	1	Correct median		Ch1.7
		(ii)	−2 and 4 4 − (−2) = 6 °C	✓ ✓	2	Correct quartiles Calculate interquartile range		Ch1.7
	c)		The median; it is closer to most of the temperatures.	✓	1	Conclusion and valid reason		Ch1.8
	d)		On average the temperatures for the last ten days are higher. The temperatures for the last ten days are more consistent.	✓ ✓	2	Valid comment regarding the mean Valid comment regarding the standard deviation	Comments must be related to the context of the question and show an understanding that mean is an average and standard deviation is a measure of spread. Simply stating that the mean is higher and the standard deviation is lower gains 0 marks.	Ch1.8
7	a)		$\pi \times 4^2 \times 15 \div 2$ $= 376.99...$ $376.99... + 8 \times 15 \times 6$ $= 376.99... + 720$ $= 1096.99...$ $= 1097\,\text{m}^3$	✓ ✓ ✓	3	Correct substitution into $\pi r^2 h \div 2$ Correct substitution into lbh and know to add to $\pi r^2 h \div 2$ Calculate volume of barn to nearest cubic metre	Remember the unit (m³).	Ch2.10
	b)		$w \times 15 \times 4 + \frac{1}{2} \times w \times 2 \times 15$ $75 \times w = 250$ $w = 250 \div 75 = 3.33...$ $\Rightarrow 3.3\,\text{m}$	✓ ✓ ✓	3	Begin to form expression for volume of extension Simplify and equate to 250 Calculate width correct to one decimal place	Remember the unit (m).	Ch2.10